Love Notes

_____

_____

PRESENTED TO:

_____

FROM:

Love Notes

My Love Note to You

_____

_____

_____

_____

_____

Love Notes

Love Notes

From
My
HEART
to
Yours

DIANNA BOOHER

Published by J. Countryman, a Division of Thomas Nelson, Inc.
Nashville, Tennessee 37214

Project Editor—Terri Gibbs

Published in association with the literary agency of Alive Communications, 1465 Kelly Johnson Blvd., Suite 320, Colorado Springs, CO 80920.

Designed by Garborg Design Works, Minneapolis, Minnesota

Illustrations by Sabra Inzer

ISBN: 0-8499-5263-8

Printed and bound in Hong Kong

Married love

encompasses

all the

attributes of

friendship—

with chocolate

on top.

Love does not consist in gazing at each other but in looking outward together in the same direction.

—Antoine de Saint-Exupery

I love you because

you always tell me

to drive carefully,

wear a coat,

get some rest,

and stop

worrying.

Why should

I worry?

I have you.

EVEN IF I HAD NEVER MET YOU, I WOULD HAVE DREAMED OF WHAT LIFE WOULD HAVE BEEN LIKE TO BE LOVED BY SUCH A PERSON LIKE YOU! *Larryson Garber*

I feel as though

you were made to

order for me.

An off-the-rack

mate would never do.

I want us to dress

up and parade

through life together

as if we were going

to a party.

Love: If you have it, you don't need anything else, and if you don't have it, it doesn't much matter what else you have.

—J. M. Barrie

You always find
a way—not an
excuse. Whatever the
predicament we find
ourselves in,
you always find a way
to resolve it,
remake it, or move
us through it.
Thank you for not
giving up.
Thank you for
being so persistent
and consistent.

What can be seen by
the eyes and heard by
the ears is nothing —
compared to what
is felt by the heart.

I LOVE YOU
WITH ALL
MY HEART!

Passion is the quickest to develop,

and the quickest to fade.

Intimacy develops more slowly,

and commitment more gradually still.

—**Robert Sternberg**

You hold my

hand and hug

me in public.

These small

gestures send a

BIG message to

the world—that

you love me.

For my sweet precious ♡

You sometimes let me have the last

word—even when it's wrong.

And when you could, you don't

take the parting shot, one that

could cut me to the quick.

When you "lose" an opportunity

like that, we both win.

I'm so grateful that divorce

is not an option with us—

that our relationship

is secure enough to

provide deep-down

assurance that

we'll stay together

until we work

things out,

no matter what.

Just seeing you makes me happy! I LOVE You!

A wedding is an event,

but marriage is an achievement.

— Anonymous

You neither try to run over me

to get your way, nor back down about

your own needs and wants.

I couldn't respect you if you always

gave in to me. And I couldn't love you

if you demanded that I always

give in to you. You negotiate

in gentleness because you're strong.

I like that.

The concept of two people living together

for twenty-five years without having

a cross word suggests a lack of spirit

only to be admired in sheep.

—A. P. Herbert

Love Notes

Thank you for appreciating me and our

love while we still have time together.

We both have looked at reality in

this crazy world and know

that we live in safety and good

health only by God's grace.

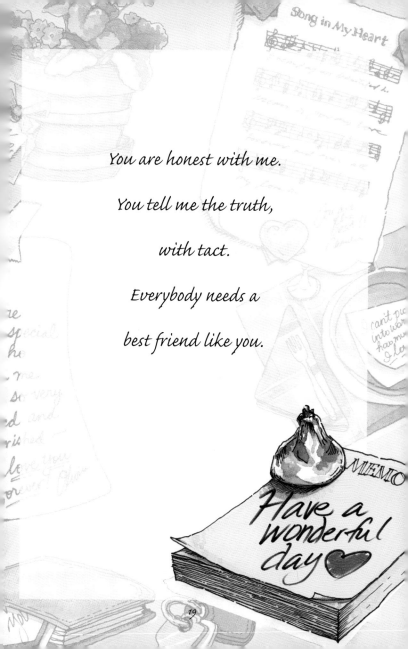

You are honest with me.

You tell me the truth,

with tact.

Everybody needs a

best friend like you.

Love doesn't make the world go 'round.

Love is what makes the ride worthwhile.

—Franklin P. Jones

I love you for

laughing with me.

You let me tease you.

Thank you for

rolling with the

punches and

the pranks.

Love you very
much · I love you
very much · I love
you very much ·
I ♥ U   I ♥ U   I ♥ U

I love you because

when there are

two pieces of banana

cream pie,

you always say

you're really

not hungry

and give me

the bigger piece.

I respect our pact of confidentiality

and so do you. You keep things

between us private. I can tell you

my deepest needs and feelings in

confidence, knowing that no one

else on this earth will hold my

secrets as safe as you.

I'm so thankful

that you have

a short memory where

failure is concerned.

You don't keep

plowing up the past.

Sure, we've had some

rough times, but we've

always moved on.

YOU ADD
SO
MUCH TO MY
LIFE!!

Love is an act of endless forgiveness,

a tender look that becomes a habit.

— **Peter Ustinov**

I love you

because you

like and

accept my

friends.

You make

these important

people a part

of our life

together.

I love you so much!

Love Notes

You make me want to do nice things for

everybody in my path. And then I like

myself better for that. I guess you could

say your love multiplies me.

Love is of all passions

the strongest, for it attacks

simultaneously the head,

the heart, and the senses.

—Voltaire

Love Notes

Living with you is like having caviar

for an appetizer, sirloin for an entree,

and crême brulée for dessert. You're a

feast that fills me up!

You are
the special
one who
makes me
feel so very
loved and
cherished —
I love you
forever! Olivia

When I'm late

getting home,

you're worried

and pacing

the floor,

looking for me

or calling

the neighbors.

Your love makes me

feel safe, cared for.

Our love began as magic;

I don't want it to end as habit.

I promise not ever to take

you for granted.

Love Notes

EVEN IF I HAD NEVER
MET YOU, I WOULD
HAVE DREAMED OF
WHAT LIFE WOULD HAVE
BEEN LIKE TO BE LOVED
BY SUCH A PERSON
LIKE YOU! Love you, darling

A successful marriage is an edifice

that must be rebuilt every day.

—André Maurois

You tell me when I've got lipstick on my tooth or my slip is showing. And you let me tell you about the toothpaste on your nose or your scratchy beard. Love is like that— concerned responsibility for another person as well as for yourself.

Prince Philip once said that when

a man opens the car door for his wife,

it's either a new car or a new wife.

I love you because that's not

true with us.

In so many

little ways, you

still treat me

like I'm special.

What can be seen by
the eyes—and heard by
ears is nothing—
compared to what
is felt by the heart.

I LOVE YOU
WITH ALL
MY HEART!

You talk to me with your eyes.

And the longer we are together,

the more languages they speak.

You make choosing a gift for me

such a big deal. You hint. You ask

what I want. You watch my eyes

light up when we shop. And somehow

you always know. But more than

the gift, I love the giver.

The supreme happiness of life

is the conviction that we are loved.

—Victor Hugo

Love makes a woman stronger

and a man gentler. Women grow more

confident and bold while men grow

more sensitive and controlled.

Talk takes time but opens my heart

to your love. Our conversations

relieve me from the stress of

everyday life—decisions, hustle

and bustle, even accomplishments.

Our talk releases my

heart into the

hands of one

who cares.

For
my
sweet
precious ♡

It takes a humble, vulnerable spirit

to talk honestly to God in front

of another person. Thank you for

letting me be that other person.

Love Notes

When you're away, you take time

to write me notes and letters and cards.

More than kisses, your written words

touch my soul. I turn each phrase over

and over in my mind

and feel each

word

caress

my heart.

Listening is the best

"line" you ever tried

with me.

You listen

to me—

with your heart,

your mind, and your soul.

You read between the lines and

ask questions to understand exactly

what I'm trying to express.

You are the special one who makes me feel so very loved and cherished—I love you forever! Olivia

Always be willing to listen

and slow to speak.

Do not become angry easily....

—James 1:19 ncv

Love Notes

You can make me forget a difficult day.

You have a way of talking my troubles

through and touching me so that every

ounce of

frustration

flows away.

K—
you light
up my
life...
xoxo

44

You're worth showing off to my family and friends. I watch you interact with those around us—asking questions, sharing your interests, laughing, and playing—and I'm proud that such a warm, witty, intriguing person chose to spend life with me.

Love Notes

I love you because you take me seriously—

you're concerned that I'm working too hard,

worrying too much, aren't appreciated

enough, or don't relax enough.

When you're so

concerned about me,

I don't have to be.

Treasure the love you receive above all.

It will survive long after your gold

and good health have vanished.

—*Og Mandino*

Love Notes

You're such a wonderful parent.

I love the way you are with

the kids—how you play with them,

tease them, encourage them,

and comfort them.

I hope they

grow up to be

just like you.

Just seeing you makes me happy!

I LOVE You!

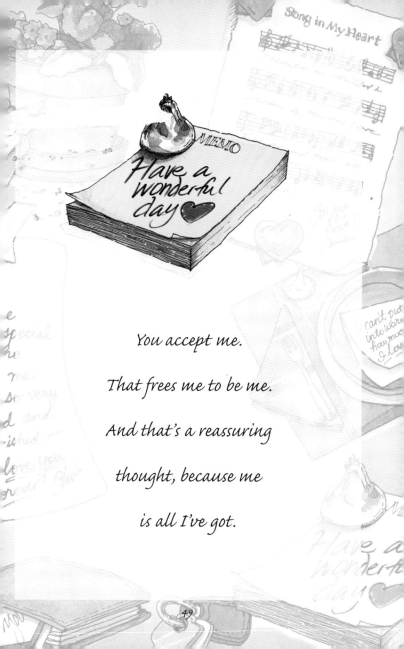

You accept me.

That frees me to be me.

And that's a reassuring

thought, because me

is all I've got.

I want not only to be loved

but to be told that I am loved.

—George Eliot

When I deserve your love the least,

that's when you give it the most.

When I'm irritable, exhausted,

discouraged, or distant, you understand.

Get along with each other,

and forgive each other.

If someone does wrong to you,

forgive that person because

the Lord forgave you.

—*Colossians 3:13 ncv*

I love you for putting anger aside,

for not holding onto it

and letting it build a gulf

between us. Thank you for

forgiving me so often.

Forgiveness clears

the way for us

to connect emotionally

once again.

Thanks for noticing the little things

I do. You always compliment me—

especially in front of other people.

And the more specific your compliments,

the more powerful the punch.

This being in love is great—

you get a lot of compliments and

begin to think you are a great guy.

—F. Scott Fitzgerald

Love Notes

Your childhood often shapes the love you

give. You've looked into your past for habits

and attitudes that are worth keeping—

and discarded those that are

tattered and torn.

Thank you for

making our love

the best of the

past and the

brightest of the new.

You understand that sometimes

I don't want praise from you—

just interest. Thank you for asking

about a difficult day and for listening

to my issues and making them

important in your life, too.

So a man will leave his father

and mother and be united with his wife,

and the two will become one body.

—Ephesians 5:31 ncv

Having sex with you is sacred.

It is more than an expression

of sexual and personal feelings;

it is an act of uniting our souls.

In real love you want the other person's good.

In romantic love you want the other person.

—**Margaret Anderson**

When we make music together,

we always seem to be singing the

same song. You can look at me when

something happens and we both know

what each of us is thinking. When you

shrug a shoulder or raise an

eyebrow, I know

what it means.

You keep me

humming in my sleep.

I love you because you can

be spontaneous. Like when we're

reading the newspaper and then,

suddenly, we're in the ice cream shop.

Or when we're cooking dinner

together and, suddenly, we're out

in the backyard watching the squirrels.

Life with you is never boring.

Love Notes

Variety is nice—in games, in music,

in tasks. But you provide all the "spice"

I need in life. You have all the

ingredients for my favorite recipe of love.

I'm so glad you are careful with our money.

It's fun to decide what we need together—

to build a comfortable home for our family.

And I love the way you splurge to buy gifts

for me. But never forget—I'd still love you

even if we lost it all.

Love Notes

You understand when I feel sad.

When I feel down about my work or

friends or for no good reason

at all, you wait

patiently

until I can

reconnect and

regain my

perspective.

What can be seen by the eyes — and heard by the ears is nothing — compared to what is felt by the heart.

I LOVE YOU WITH ALL MY HEART!

You love my family. You've accepted them;

you treat them with as much love and

respect as your own—and they don't

always deserve it. That reminds me all

over again how big

your heart is.

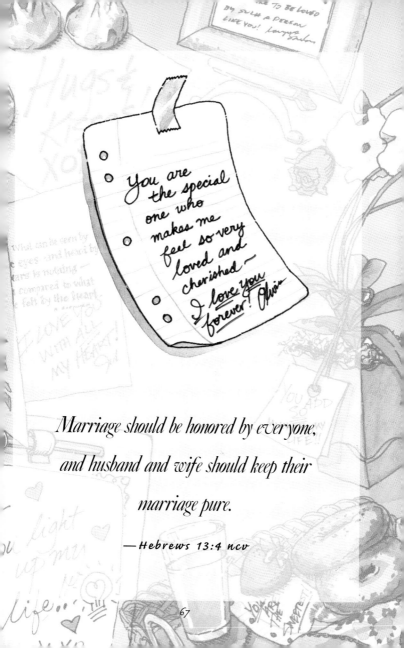

You are
the special
one who
makes me
feel so very
loved and
cherished —
I love you
forever! Olivia

Marriage should be honored by everyone,

and husband and wife should keep their

marriage pure.

—Hebrews 13:4 ncv

You've committed your love to me forever.

Our decision to stay together—

through money crises, kids crises,

or corporate cutbacks—provides an

inner security that nobody can shake.

Love Notes

It feels good to have you as an ally. You take my side on issues. You show your loyalty when others are "putting in their two cents' worth." Could you possibly agree with me all those times? I don't think so.

If we were keeping

score, you'd be

winning by a

million to one.

You put your love

in action. Like

running my bath

water . . . washing

the car . . . bringing

me iced tea.

Love has nothing to do with
what you are expecting to get—
only with what you are expecting
to give—which is everything.

—Katherine Hepburn

Love Notes

Thank you for

letting me sit

in solitude

sometimes—

without asking

what's wrong.

I love the way we

can sit quietly

together

and feel

comfortable.

I feel successful in life.

Winning your love is

my greatest achievement.

When we sleep in each other's arms,

we fit together like spoons.

We melt into each other's souls.

Nights were made for this.

You celebrate my successes with me. I can't brag to my bosses. I can't brag to my friends. I can't brag to the neighbors. But with you, I can SHOUT it from the mountaintops and you'll climb along with me.

Love Notes

Happiness makes a person smile,

but sadness can break a person's spirit.

—*Proverbs 15:13 ncv*

Watching you laugh gives me so

much joy. I love the way your eyes

start to dance, the corners of your

smile spread, and your face lights up.

I know it's not easy to point out

somebody's blind spots. You do it

ever so gently, with my best interest

at heart. You are willing to risk

my anger by trying to help me

change for the better. Thank you for

caring enough to do that.

Love Notes

You take care of yourself for me.

You stay healthy, dress tastefully,

and recharge your energy.

I love the way you look.

Just seeing you makes me happy!

I LOVE You!

You are not afraid to ask for love and compassion when you need it. Thank you for admitting that you need my love.

EVEN IF I HAD NEVER MET YOU, I WOULD HAVE DREAMED OF WHAT LIFE WOULD HAVE BEEN LIKE TO BE LOVED BY SUCH A PERSON LIKE YOU! Love, Sabin

At parties and get-togethers

you show your love openly.

This builds my trust in you.

I feel safe because others

know you are committed to me.

The critical period in matrimony

is breakfast time.

—A. P. Herbert

You care enough to keep the romance alive. Thank you for taking time to have fun with me, to plan our nights out, our weekends, our vacations.

YOU ADD SO MUCH TO MY LIFE!!

Love Notes

You welcome me home when I've been

away, even for a day. I love it when you

stop what you're doing and come to say

"I've missed you." That makes me eager

to get back to you

the next time . . .

and the next.

You read my mind and my moods.

When my body language or expression

says I'm dejected, you probe

with questions, "Say, you look sad . . .

happy . . . frustrated. Want to tell

me about it?" Do you know what

a blessed invitation that is?

Sex is a three-letter word

that sometimes needs some old-fashioned

four-letter words to convey its full meaning—

words like help, give, care, love.

—Sam Levenson

Love Notes

The way you touch me still sends chills down my spine. You make me feel exciting, charming, erotic. Your caresses stir passion that can't be expressed in words. Come to think of it, I guess that's why God created sex.

You focus on the solution rather than

the problem. Sometimes I get caught

up in the argument and can't see the

resolution for the answer. Thanks for

not letting us get stuck there.

We have so much fun with

other happy couples in love.

Sometimes you feel close to

one of the pair; sometimes

I feel close to one of the pair.

In either case, you make the

foursome fit. That doubles

our fun together.

You haven't made me

live up—or down—

to your expectations.

It's as if you walked into

this relationship

and tossed all

previous

expectations

to the wind. That

has given me such

freedom to be me.

I love how you work at helping me fulfill

my personal goals. You care that I learn

new things, meet new people, share new

experiences. I feel like you care about my

personal growth as much as your own.

You enjoy each day.

Yes, of course, I'm happy that

you look to the future with

plans, but I'm grateful that

we don't miss living together

each day.

I told you I loved you the day we got married.

If I change my mind, I'll let you know.

—Anonymous

You are
the special
one who
makes me
feel so very
loved and
cherished—
I love you
forever! Olivia

I am puzzled and intrigued:

Which feels better—to love or

to be loved by you? It may

take a lifetime to find out.

Love Notes

Kiss me with the kisses of your mouth,

because your love is better than wine.

—Song of Solomon 1:2

Humor helps heal hurt.

We laugh a lot together.

That feels deep down good.

Let's do it more often.

You are honest and
strong enough to tell
me what you think.
I can trust you to be
truthful. Playing
guessing games
can be much too
dangerous in love.

What can be seen by
e eyes—and heard by
ars is nothing—
compared to what
e felt by the heart.

I LOVE YOU
WITH ALL
MY HEART!

The pleasure of love is in loving.

We are happier in the passion

we feel than in that we arouse.

—La Rochefoucauld

Love Notes

When I see you walk

into a room,

I feel excited,

supported, protected,

cherished—completed.

Rather than being sapped by problems,

our love gives energy to solutions.

You always try to

come up with

the right

answers.

K—
you light
up my
life...!!
XOXO

They say there is a book in every

marriage. Ours is a Little Golden

Book with a happy ending—

and a happy beginning and a

happy middle.

Love Notes

Goethe said, "We learn from only those we love." Because I feel your love so deeply, I have learned much of life from you. You are my teacher in so many ways.

MEMO

Have a wonderful day ♥

Your love feels like a warm

coat on a cold night.

Whatever weather I walk

through, you're there to

surround and protect me.

I love it that you flirt with me—after all

these years. I love how you reach out and

pat me when no one's looking. I love the

twinkle in your eyes when you tease me.

Flirting adds flavor to the main course.

I can't put
into words
how much
I Love you!

You are strong enough to be tender.

I'm grateful that you see the world with

sensitivity and try in small ways every

day to make it better for somebody else.

Love Notes

We two form a multitude.

—*Ovid*

Thank you for trusting me

to raise our children—

to shape them, guide them,

sometimes decide for them.

I promise never to betray

that trust but

always to instill

in them respect and

love for you.

YOU ADD
SO
MUCH TO MY
LIFE!!

Love Notes

I thank my God every time

I remember you. . . .

— **Philippians 1:3**

I love how you make God first place

in our lives. I know that our faith will

hold us together in tough times,

and I rest secure that you are seeking

His leadership for our lives.

There is no more lovely,

friendly and charming relationship,

communion or company than a

good marriage.

—Martin Luther